Hip-Hop Verse Shakespeare's Othello

"WHEN THE KNIGHT FELL" V.1
CLEAR RISES

Christopher Gary Simmons

Copyright © 2025 by Christopher Gary Simmons.

All rights reserved. No part of this book may be reproduced in any form or by any electronic or mechanical means, including information storage and retrieval systems, without permission in writing from the author Christopher Gary Simmons, and only for excepts by reviewers to quote brief passages in reviews.

This publication contains the opinions and ideas of the author. It is intended to provide helpful and informative material on the subjects addressed in the publication. The author denies all responsibility for any liability, loss, or risk, personal or otherwise, which is incurred as a consequence, directly or indirectly, of the use and application of any of the contents of this book.

Hip-Hop Verse Shakespeare's Othello:

Contact Author: 1-267-977-5900
Email: christophergarysimmons@gmail.com
Website: www.hiphopverseshakespeare.com

Ordering Information (Quantity Sales):
(For details contact the author at the address or *number above.)*
Discounts available on quantity purchases by Theaters, Colleges, Universities, Public Schools, Corporations, Associations & Others.

Library of Congress Control Number: TX0009412133

ISBN: 9798312543988 [Paperback | Digital]

Table of Contents:

Audio # 01 | Introduction

Act 1 Content

Page 1: Audio # 02 | **Act 1 Scene 1**

Page 2: Audio # 03 | *"Halfway Shook"*

Page 10: Audio # 04 | **Act 1 Scene 2**

Page 11: Audio # 05 | *"A Clear Knight"*

Page 15: Audio # 06 | **Act 1 Scene 3A**

Page 16: Audio # 07 | *"The Gathering"*

Page 23: Audio # 08 | **Act 1 Scene 3B**

Page 24: Audio # 09 | *"No Angel"*

Page 28: Audio # 10 | **Act 1 Scene 3C**

Page 29: Audio # 11 | *"Put Money On It"*

Act 2 Content

Page 33: Audio # 12 | **Act 2 Scene 1A**

Page 35: Audio # 13 | *"Homecoming"*

Page 40: Audio # 14 | **Act 2 Scene 1B**

Page 41: Audio # 15 | *"Art of Words"*

Page 47: Audio # 16 | **Act 2 Scene 1C**

Page 48: Audio # 17 | *"Still Shady"*

Page 51: Audio # 18 | **Act 2 Scene 2**

Page 52: Audio # 19 | *"NUZEE Luv Ballad"*

Page 53: Audio # 20 | **Act 2 Scene 3A**

Page 54: Audio # 21 | *"Club Castle"*

Page 59: Audio # 22 | **Act 2 Scene 3B**

Page 61: Audio # 23 | *"War Party"*

Act 3 Content

Page 68: Audio # 24 | **Act 3 Scene 1**

Page 69: Audio # 25 | *"Jealous Never Worry"*

Page 72: Audio # 26 | **Act 3 Scene 2**

Page 73: Audio # 27 | *"Worry Less"*

Page 74: Audio # 28 | **Act 3 Scene 3A**

Page 75: Audio # 29 | *"The Big Approach"*

Page 79: Audio # 30 | **Act 3 Scene 3B**

Page 81: Audio # 31 | *"Thin Air"*

Page 88: Audio # 32 | **Act 3 Scene 3C**

Page 90: Audio # 33 | *"Sour Candy"*

Page 93: Audio # 34 | **Act 3 Scene 3D**

Page 94: Audio # 35 | *"Something Unsaid"*

Page 98: Audio # 36 | **Act 3 Scene 3E**

Page 99: Audio # 37 | *"Mind Games"*

Closing Content

Page 103: Ayatul Kursi

Page 104: Clear's Intermission

Page 105: WTKF Audiobook | Access & Promotion

Page 106: WTKF Audiobook | Literary Musical Playlist

Page 107: WTKF Audiobook | Performance Playlist

Characters inspired by Othello & Hip-Hop Artists

Clear	Othello - *Eminem*
Diamond	Desdemona - *Nicki Minaj*
Tio	Brabantio - *Ice Cube*
Ego	Iago - *The Industry*
Millie	Emilia - *Missy*
Bee	Bianca - *Eve*
Mike Cash	Michael Cassio - *Kendrick Lamar*
Ar *(Rodrique)*	Rodrigo - *Yaseen Bay*
Duke	The Duke of Venice - *50 Cent*
Justice	First Senator - *Nas*
Rock	Second Senator - *Q-Tip*
Toni	Montano - *T.I.*
Grant	Gratiano - *Busta Rhymes*

Characters inspired by Othello & Hip-Hop Artists

Lock		**Lodovico -** *Dr. Dre*
Pierce		**The First Gentlemen -** *Andre 3000*
Hunter		**The Second Gentlemen -** *Big Boi*
Angel		**The Third Gentlemen -** *Ludacris*
Bike Courier		**The Sailor -** *Lil Wayne*
Phone Calls		**Messengers -** *MC Lyte & Common*
Erica Herald		**The Herald -** *Lauryn Hill*
Stretch		**Clown -** *Snoop Dogg*
Bass		**Musicians -** *Method Man & Redman*
Blackman		**Othello's Servant -** *Black Thought*
911		**Brabantio's Servant -** *Queen Latifah*
Music		**Officers -** *Timbaland & Pharrell*

Audio # 01 | Introduction & Dedication

In the name of God, the entirely merciful, the especially merciful. May this book help protect us from the mistakes our egos make and serve as a form of Sadaqah Jariyah for all who read and share it...

"WHEN THE KNIGHT FELL"

Dedicated to my baby sister,

- Talia Anunca Dubose

Thank you for always inspiring me to do better.

I miss you. I love you forever. For Ottwatt...

Audio # 02 | <u>**Act 1 Scene 1**</u>

This story begins and ends with a small clique of music industry friends. For them, this moment in time could have been early spring, late nineties. Each of them feeling like it was an idyllic time to be alive. In lower Manhattan near Chinatown, on an empty cobblestone street off Canal, two young men from this talented faction engage in a heated conversation. Holding court beneath the light of the setting sun, one of the men named Ar is upset. His friend Ego, however, is resting comfortably against a parking kiosk. Both men adorn a tasteful amount of jewelry to complement their fashionable attire. Parked next to them is a new sparkling black S.U.V. The hazard lights from the truck flicker on and off continuously in the twilight. While the men exchange words, the sun falls toward the west and the natural daylight sinks below the towering skyscrapers.

A crimson-colored sky surrenders power to an ocean of countless nightlights and streetlamps. An artificial glow now illuminates the streets and high lofty buildings of the New York night. The two men continue talking as they take their conversation into the confines of the truck. Ar speeds off in a hurry. They head across the Brooklyn Bridge and park on a block in Crown Heights lined with well-kept brownstones. With Ar brandishing a small pistol, they exit the truck and take cover behind the vehicle, huddling on the pavement next to the rear tire. Hidden from view by the evening shadows, Ego takes out his cell phone and makes a call. Ar hesitantly fires his weapon in the air. Following the sound of the shots, a bedroom light comes on in a house across from the truck.

A man named Tio inside the house answers Ego's call and they launch into a frantic back and forth exchange. Ar listens nervously with his ear pressed against the back of Ego's phone. When Ar finally inserts himself into the conversation, Tio immediately recognizes the sound of his voice. Using the barrel of a large handgun, Tio parts his curtains and opens his bedroom window. At the same time, Ego pushes Ar from behind the truck unexpectedly. Tio sees him and points the gun in his direction.

Ar looks up to find a small red laser extending from Tio's firearm to his chest and fearfully takes cover behind the truck again. Tio hangs up the phone and rushes into the bedroom across the hall. While he is distracted, Ar stands up once more in full view of the window and Ego slips off into the darkness. Shocked to find his daughter's room empty, Tio dials 911 and returns to the open window. He shouts angrily down at Ar on the street below, ordering him to help his bodyguards search for and find his missing daughter Diamond.

Audio # 03 | *"Halfway Shook"*

Ar and Ego stand beneath a New York city streetlamp -

Ar: *How did you get me into this? Your rep is infamous.*

He'll know it's us. He'll find out then he'll murder us.

Who said I was equipped for warfare with Clear?

His tolerance for violence, stays up in the air.

It's getting late. I need to know if my money's straight.

Ego: *Well, cut to the chase. Stab my brain with my nose plate.*

We either catch a break or catch a case. Tempt fate.

Why wait? You came to me for God's sake.

Ar: *Why is everything with Clear, so love / hate?*

Ego: *On everything, I want to stick my gun in his face.*

I'll cock back the hammer. Make him show me the safe.

Put the barrel in his mouth, so I can show him his place.

He's proud right now. He shows work, they show love.

I'm like, "Cert set me up?" and get the MJ glove.

They won't touch me, but they're putting him on.

Mike Cash does his math, so his money is long.

He talks to models, whips a Benz, pops bottles.

Never pulled a trigger while smashing a throttle.

I have seen dirt from inner-city to outskirts.

When I'm putting in work, more than feelings get hurt.

How is a soldier with no scars, put above me?

How did he position himself with Clear so lovely?

Trust me, when his payday comes it will get ugly.

Ar: *Lift him off the planet, with a slug in his frame.*

Ego: *If it were that simple, I would have some love in this game.*

Ar: *If I'm hearing what you're saying you're aiming to turn on him.*

Ego and Ar enter a car and drive off -

Ego: *Not so fast. First, we learn on him. Master his craft.*

Fill his head up with gas. Follow his path. Feed him with flames,

That burn on him. All that respect Clear had, I will get that.

Play like his right-hand man and then flip that.

Sit back. Watch how most men make it.

Anything in this world, if you want it, you better take it.

Put your game down, and lace it. I'm that type.

While I have you in my corner, I am set for life.

If Clear wasn't here I could handle his wealth.

For now, I follow him and look ahead for myself.

I have the ace of hearts up my sleeve. I'm at ease.

I'm exactly what I am, but not exactly what I seem.

Ar: *What has to happen for us to make a come up?*

Ego and Ar arrive in front of Tio's house and exit the car -

Ego: *Get in front of her dad's house and throw your gun up.*

Lick off shots in the air. Wake everyone up.

Tell Tio, Diamond's with Clear before sun-up.

Ar: *Her people live right over here.*

Ego places a phone call to Tio -

Ego: *Time to bust off.*

Ar shoots his gun in the air and ducks behind the car with Ego -

Ar: Let the streets tell it.

Ego: Let the streets tell it.

Inside the house Tio answers the phone call from Ego -

Ar: Let the streets tell it. Your daughter is 'bout to run off.

Tio: Is this the man in front of my house, letting the gun off?

Ar: Is all your family home, and your alarms on?

Tio: Is this a dead man talking to me on the phone?

Ego: You're missing one of your valuable jewels. Man, get up.

Tio: Whoever this is will get split quick and lit up.

Ego: Think about your daughter, legs split, giving it up.

Tio: Is this Ron?

Ego stifles his laughter as he pretends to be Ar over the phone -

Ego: No, Rodrique.

Tio: You little geek. My daughters' too sweet for the street.

She's no freak. After this stunt, believe me you won't eat.

You're time's up in this city. Blow the scene.

Before I strobe light this block with a red beam.

Ar: I know what I've seen. Diamond's out on the creep!

Tio: Why should I believe your motive is pure peace?

Ar: The streets will feast on Diamond, to say the least.

Ego: The situation is bleak. She's in it waist deep.

Tio: Is this really you Rodrique?

Ego: Don't sleep. Your daughter's on her back with a beast,

In silk sheets.

Tio: My daughter's never been that weak. You're out of bounds.

Ego: Perception is reality. Word gets around.

Tio: I have a long reach Rodrique, so cease now.

Either keep it moving, or speak your peace now.

Ar: I'm not pressed for money. You know it deep down.

The last thing I'm trying to catch is a beat down.

Whatever's lost can be found, so look now.

Do you really know where your daughter is right now?

Tio finds his daughter's bedroom empty and calls 911 -

Police: 911, Emergency...

Tio: Yes, my daughter's missing.

Police: *Has it been 24 hours?*

Tio: *Listen. Check your position.*

I'm a friend of the mayor.

I will sue your division.

Ego speaks to Ar from behind the car then exits into the dark -

Ego: *Look... I have to be gone. You have to be strong.*

I have to act as if I'm in it with Clear from now on,

And even though I hate him to death, with hate on my breath,

I'll talk as if I love him, then play him like chess.

Just bring Tio out to his rest ready to flex.

I'll play his right hand. You play his left and we'll be set.

Tio: *It's all too true, the evil that men do.*

Somebody has to know something.

Why would she act a fool?

Ar: *I hear she's been hanging with Clear.*

Maybe it's true.

Aside -

Tio: Heavenly father, what's a father supposed to do?

One second out of my view, now my Diamond's in the rough.

Ar shouts up to Tio's window -

Ar: She's grown up enough, that it doesn't take much.

Tio returns to his phone conversation with Ar -

Tio: All right, I've heard enough. Time for shaking things up.

Ar: You know what? I know where they're holding up, but trust.

Clear will go in hard on whoever shows up.

Tio: I'll send three of my thugs, killers with cold blood.

If Clears with her, then I want his spot blown up.

Audio # 04 | **Act 1 Scene 2**

Later that evening, Clear and Ego meet in front of the Ritz Carlton across from Central Park. A valet driver pulls up to the hotel in a Range Rover and exits the vehicle. Clear walks over and gives the young man a generous tip in exchange for the keys to the truck. He then returns to chatting with Ego beneath the lights of the hotel entrance.

A small Mercedes Benz races toward them and catches all of their attention. The car comes to a screeching halt in front of the building. Clear's good friend and business partner Michael Cash springs out from the driver's side. Happy to see each other, Clear greets Cash with a big brotherly hug and invites him to join the conversation with Ego.

Not too long after Cash's arrival, another vehicle shows up carrying Ar, Tio and three of his bodyguards. Clear walks back over to the Range Rover still parked at the curb. He reaches through the open window of the truck and pulls a gun from the glove box. He tucks the weapon into a holster at the small of his back. He then turns toward the group of hostile men approaching him, prepared to confront them with violence if necessary.

Audio # 05 | *"A Clear Knight"*

Ego and Clear stand at the entrance of an apartment building -

Ego: *I've seen war before, put metal through many men.*

I let hollow tips rip through flesh with no conscience.

I hear Tio's causing you problems. I can solve them.

Clear: *Let it be what it is.*

I'm one to forgive.

Ego: *Let this man live, he'll trash your name.*

Every word out his mouth, he's been asking for pain.

If you really married his daughter, you're back in the game.

Your status will change. As soon as you change your status,

All the lawyers will just double up and come back at us.

Then anytime you make a move, out come the soldiers.

One word, "Annulment." They'll want to expose you.

Everyone will tell her she should wait until she's older.

Clear: *They can talk it. You know I talk, live and walk it.*

They know I'm thick with green, my team's cash is hitting.

I've been from gutter to butter leather and fast whipping.

From a thoroughbred position, I'll make the world listen.

My mission is to show I love Diamond to death.

Until my dying breath, God knows I'm blessed,

With a lot more heart than chest. You know my rep.

Ego spots someone approaching -

Ego: That's her father and his crew,

Coming at you with the screw face. You should go.

Come on. Be gone. Get your boots laced.

Clear: What, run? Let them come and bring their guns.

Right now, my mind, my body and soul are one,

And hold my tongue is something I will not do.

I will speak true. Then we'll have to see who's who.

Ego: Wait son, that's not Tio. That's Cash's Benz.

Clear: The lieutenant, I would never Clash with him.

Cash what's up? What has dipping out in the cut?

Cash: To let you know what's up. Duke needs a general.

He has a job for you, that only few men will do.

Clear: Am I wanted or needed?

Cash: Well the business is heated.

It sounds rather ugly, so that is how I would treat it.

My street team is spreading the word.

We all heard. Duke is ready to merge, with major men.

Clear: *No doubt. It's good to know what phase he's in.*

O.K. Give me a second. Let me call up the house,

Speak with the spouse, gain four pounds and we can bounce.

Cash: *What's that all about? You're talking like your wifed-up.*

Ego: *His marriage vows are out. He just changed his life up.*

Cash: *I don't understand.*

Ego*: Your friend is a married man.*

Cash: *How in the world did he settle for that scam?*

Ego: *We'll talk about it later.*

Clear, what's the plan?

Clear: *Nothing's changed. Different day, same routine.*

We need to do a little dirty work and come out clean.

Cash sees another group of men approaching -

Cash: *Clear watch your back.*

Who are these shady cats?

Rolling in a pack. Carrying straps.

Heavily stacked.

Clear: *Stand down!!! Before I put you and your man down.*

How you want to figure this out? It's in your hands now.

Tio: *You know the story.*

No guts no glory.

Clear: *Now is not the time. You're thinking too poorly.*

I have some other serious business standing before me.

Cash: *That's a fact. Ease back.*

What he's saying is true.

We have a meeting with Duke,

At his office, at 2:00 am.

Tio: *I'll make sure Duke's only concern is you.*

I attend all meetings that concern his crew.

We'll go to his office together. If he no shows,

I off you and toss you, cut your throat slow,

You'll quickly find out about me, what you don't know.

Audio #6 | Act 1 Scene 3A

Inside the Time Warner Center building, a music mogul named Duke sits in his boardroom with two unofficial business partners. The mahogany furniture and plush carpets in his office space are spotless. Even at 2:00 am the massive windows in the boardroom offer a picturesque view of Columbus Circle below. Frosted sliding glass doors cover the entire entrance side of the dimly lit room. An attractive young female friend of Duke's sits in the lobby outside the space. She swings back and forth at the receptionist's desk, playing on her phone. The desk is backed by an indoor fountain that extends to the ceiling. Above the rippling water hangs the portrait of a record company logo. It displays a bullet riddled dog tag with the words "War Torn Music" engraved across it.

The lobby in front of the desk which would be bustling with activity during the day is empty and silent at this late hour. Two guards stand posted inside the glass doors of the lobby entrance. Their eyes are fixed on the elevator bank in the hallway just outside the office doors. Inside the boardroom, Duke and his two companions discuss a number of important business matters. They are seated together at one end of a long wooden conference table. With every gesture, beams of light reflect across the ceiling, glittering off the diamonds in Duke's bracelet. A bike courier enters the room timidly. Duke signs for the delivery of a leather bag and the courier exits after a few parting words. Duke empties the contents of the designer bag onto the table. It contains documents, a few pictures and some stacks of $100 bills.

The young woman in the lobby breaks into the conversation between the three men using the intercom on the boardroom phone. She impatiently informs Duke of a call he is being asked to take. She hangs up abruptly after putting the caller through to the small speaker at the center of the table. Upon seeing Clear enter the room, Duke ends his call after a few brief words. Tio strolls in ominously behind Clear. He silently walks over to the office window looking disinterested and aloof. The others are uncertain if Tio is staring at his reflection in the glass or gazing down at Central Park. Clear takes a seat at the table. Tio finally turns away from the window to speak, moving assuredly toward the center of the table directly across from Clear. They stare each other down from opposite sides of the room and engage in a tense verbal exchange. The large conference table sits like a chasm between them.

Audio #7 | *"The Gathering"*

Inside an office boardroom near Columbus Circle -

Duke: *From what I hear these so-called soldiers,*

Want to hurt something.

Justice: *I'd say out 100 only 7,*

Could be worth something.

Duke: *They would need at least 140,*

To murk something.

Rock: *The last number that I got was 200...*

Whether it's right or not, somebody wants you hunted.

Duke: *No question. It could be more or less men.*

Now is not the time for us to start resting.

Rock: *Whatever this is please be quick with your business.*

Bike Courier: *Your man Angel said, "Make sure you get this."*

For the next, 24 hrs... You're on a hit list.

Courier Exits -

Duke: *It seems as if the point of attack has shifted.*

Justice: We know about the bounty. Now, how do we lift it?

And keep all exposure to your enemies restricted?

Defensive postures become, quickly predictive.

To carry out a hit list, that takes skill.

The price to get it done right... say, half a mil.

Money makes it easy to kill, and so the danger is real;

And if they get to the head, well it's a done deal.

Duke: They don't have what it takes to get it done.

Intercom phone buzzes -

Phone call line one.

Phone: If there's a chink in your armor, they're trying to find one.

Traps have been set. We don't know who's behind them.

The first will be an ambush, probably a blind one.

Justice: Find them... and tell us how many are coming?

Phone: I'll say about 30 and they're ready and gunning,

But your man Montana said, "He has your back."

He'll watch your stacks and all he wants is props for that.

Duke: So this is how it begins? Is Lucky in the city?

Justice: No, he's down in Jersey, working Atlantic City.

Duke: Get in touch with him quickly. Tell him to get with me.
Tell him my situation is far from pretty.

Justice: Here comes Clear, Tio, and the whole committee.

Enter Clear, Ego, Cash and Tio with his men -

Duke: Clear, you're finally here. Things are getting thick.
I have some bad business, and I need you in the mix.
Tio, I didn't see you. I could use legal advice,
But I didn't want to call you in the middle of the night.

Tio: I understand. I just need to set something right.
I'm here as a father and not a lawyer tonight.

Duke: Please speak on the matter.

Tio: It's my daughter.

Rock: Is she dead?

Tio: Well I found out she's been sharing her bed.
With a thug who's got her drugged up to get an edge.

Duke: Put a name to this lame that disgraced your daughter.

And I'll give the order, put this man underground for you.

Tio: Here he is Mr. Clear S. Waters.

Who you intend to send work with,

Over the border.

Justice: Clear wouldn't do that.

Rock: Mess with your daughter?

Duke: Let him speak for himself.

Tio: If he lies let him be slaughtered.

Clear: Let me begin by respecting you O.G.s.

I'll admit that I kept things low key. The streets built me.

If marrying this old man's daughter is a crime, bottom line,

I'm guilty. See I'm the hood type. Never been the good type.

Truth is, I was born far from the good life,

I could have any woman I want on a good night.

I'd be the last one to drug up a good wife.

God strike me down if I'm lying. With a small bit of ice,

I won the heart of a Diamond.

Tio: *Why would my daughter even think to move,*

In any direction that would link her to you.

Duke: *Come on Clear,*

Connect truth to it

Justice: *Is this love legit?*

Or did you wrongly pursue it?

Clear: *Listen closely, instead of being one-sided.*

Why not let her tell you herself exactly what I did?

And if what I'm saying is false, I won't run off.

Right here and right now, you can take my head off.

Intercom: *Diamond's out here at the desk.*

Duke: *Somebody get her.*

Clear: *I will tell you what happened, before you peak with her.*

The story I will tell you is more sweet than bitter.

It only took one look, to fall in love with her.

Duke: *Clear, please make the picture,*

Much bigger.

Clear: *Her father "showed love." Invited me to his clubs.*

He brought me over his crib. He showed me how he lived.

And he constantly asked me about my past.

The kind of guns I blast, and the funds I had.

All the deadly situations that had crossed my path.

How I started on the block selling rock,

How I got locked up by the cops,

Served time in some rough spots.

How I came right back to the streets.

I was constantly, living in a man-eat-man world,

Until the homegirl put me back on my feet,

And introduced me to an M.C. I started as a bodyguard

And stick with it. Did tours around the world and saw digits.

Her father was my lawyer, and whenever I would visit,

Diamond's eyes would fix on where I was sitting.

Sometimes, we would be alone for a minute.

That's when, she would explain how my hidden,

Pain changed what she thought was God given.

Considering everything in the life she was living,

It was strange. She told me all I needed was wife.

A woman who would listen to my plight,

A woman who would see me for the knight that I was,

And for a friend like me, she would show nothing but love.

And love is all I showed to pursue her. Here she comes now.

Let her crown me or show me the sewer.

Duke: *If it's like that, not even my daughter could fight that.*

Even if I kept her from it she would go right back.

When love strikes like that, why strike back?

Tio: *For all the fatherly skills I think I might lack.*

I pray my daughter didn't play any part in this,

Art of deception and if so I'm less than,

The man and the father that I claim to be,

Let her explain to me, how this came to be.

Audio #8 | <u>Act 1 Scene 3B</u>

Clear sits motionless with his eyes closed, gathering himself. The voices of the men around him explode into a chaotic debate regarding his relationship with Diamond. The young woman still seated out at the front desk, interrupts their conversation once again using the intercom. In a contemptible tone, she notifies them that Diamond has arrived and is in the lobby waiting to speak with her father. One of Tio's guards exits the room to greet Diamond and escort her back into the boardroom.

The few seconds it takes for her to enter the room feel long and heavy. Tio glances over at Clear with an expression filled with hurt and resentment. He turns his attention back to the window in order to avoid further revealing his emotions when he sees his daughter. Diamond floats gracefully into the room. All the men's voices fall silent. She smiles at Clear then focuses her eyes on her father. In a firm but delicate voice, she addresses him confidently, even though she is the only woman in a room full of immensely powerful men.

Audio #9 | *"No Angel"*

Diamond enters a room of all men with a defiant confidence -

Diamond: Daddy, you have me so deeply divided. When I felt unsure,
You gave me guidance. Money, cars and clothes; education provided.
My respect is yours and I can't deny it, but let me make this clear,
I'm with Clear. So my heart belongs to; this over here. I chose this,
The same way, mommy chose you. I still love my daddy,
But I love Clear too.

Tio: God be with you. As of now I'm through with you.
Duke finish your business. Diamond, I dismiss you.
I'm glad that I only have one. God forgive you.
I'm glad that you weren't a son. God forbid you.

Duke: Take this small suggestion as good advice.
If you love each other, don't take this light.
Shakespeare said, **"When all the grief has ended,
By seeing the worst which late on hopes depended.
To mourn a mischief that is past and gone,
Is the next way to draw new mischief on.
What can't be preserved when fortune takes,
Patience, her injury a mockery makes.
The robbed that smiles, steals something from the thief;
He robs himself that spends a bootless grief."**

Tio: So even though it feels like I'm lost, I smile.

Even though it still feels like I've lost my child.

Duke: Give it a while. Right now, let's talk about Turk.

He needs to be reminded that he can be hurt.

Will your new wife allow you to set up shop?

And can she handle the fact, that you might be shot.

Clear: You know how I rock. Ya'll know me well.

You won't surprise me, if ya'll show me hell.

The only thing I ask if I lose my life,

Please make sure no one can abuse my wife.

Duke: So scratch plans with her father.

Tio: I wouldn't even bother.

Clear: Neither would I.

Diamond: I back that with full pride.

Duke: That means you want to be where?

Diamond: I belong with Clear. Wherever he needs care,
I will be right there. For him, there is little that I will not do.
And with all due respect, must I answer to you?

Clear: Well you see she can speak for herself a touch.
This is serious business. I treat it as such.

Duke: On that, you and your wife decide what's right.

Rock: Whatever your decision, your plane leaves tonight.

Clear: Am I taking all the brave hearts?

Duke: Leave one behind. For everybody else,
Tomorrow morning at 9:00 am. Meet back here.

Clear: Death's not a fear. On that I'm sincere.
Please tell your people, I leave my life... my wife
And trust here with Ego.

Duke: Let me say one last thing before we go.
Tio, I suggest you respect the flow,
Of a son-in-law that will take on any foe.

Justice: This queen on your hands has much love to show.

Tio: That fake love will grow. Soon you'll see,

The same dirt thrown in your eyes she tossed at me.

Clear, Diamond, Cash and Ego exit the boardroom -

Clear: My life's on it. Everything I am, has my wife on it.

Now it's on Ego. He knows I had to fight for it.

I leave my queen with my second in charge.

Leaving for overseas now, will be hard.

Give me a minute to solicit this, with Allah,

And whatever time is left, Diamond that's all yours.

Audio #10 | <u>Act 1 Scene 3C</u>

Duke and his companions acknowledge Clear with smiles as he exits the room followed by Diamond, Cash, Ego and Ar a few steps behind. Quietly, the group board an elevator outside the office together. They spill out from its doors laughing hysterically when it reaches the lobby floor. The five of them part ways after exiting the building. Clear, Diamond and Cash walk toward the park. Ego and Ar politely wave goodbye to the others and head off toward the lights of Time Square. They walk along the crowded streets of the theater district and discuss their shared disappointment in the evening.

They finally end up at 42nd street station where they board a northbound train going uptown toward Ego's home. The train reaches a stop in Harlem and the doors open next to them. Ego smiles and without saying a word steps off the train while Ar continues to ramble on. The doors close between them, cutting short their conversation. Inexplicably, Ar flashes a thumbs up sign at Ego through the window, running clumsily along the platform as the train moves on to the next stop. Ego exits the station and pauses. He takes a deep breath, looks around as if he is not sure which direction he wants to go. He shrugs apathetically, turns in the direction of the Apollo, and walks off aimlessly down 125th Street.

Audio #11 | *"Put Money on It"*

Ar and Ego break from the others and head south on Broadway -

Ar: Yo, Ego?

Ego: How is my man Rodrigo?

Ar: What do we do now? From here, where do we go?

Ego: Take yourself to bed.

Ar: I'd much rather be dead.

Ego: I wouldn't cry at your funeral, I would laugh instead.

Ar: I wouldn't even blame you. This is too painful.
Death seems to be the best place for the shameful.

Ego: Cowboy, buckle up. You're not thinking rough enough.
I've been around the block. You really need to toughen up.
Most men wouldn't know love, if it stuck him up,
In a dark alley and cut him from the guts up.
To luck up or buck up, there's a big difference.
Before I'd ever take my life over a chicken,
I would trade positions, with a foul living,
One-legged monkey trying to swim with bad vision.

Ar: If that's how I get in, tell me what to do.

I want to be less like me, and more like you.

Ego: There's only one thing in this world that can hurt you,

Trying to have virtue, to be this or that,

This life is a garden, where things grow to distract...

Your mind from your will, from what's "really real,"

From work to play, to everyday sex appeal.

Ar: It's that simple is it?

Ego: Ar you don't get it.

You only have one life to live. Now live it.

Put money on it. Think how to disguise yourself.

Put money on it. Diamond can't deny her wealth.

My wager is that she will surprise herself.

Put money on it. Things won't feel the same,

Once he gets out of the game, and things start to change,

I bet, Diamond will be the first person he blames.

Put money on it. Right now she looks so sweet.

When things get bitter, I figure he will seek,

Fresh new fruit to eat. He's straight street,

And she's young meat but he's not treating her right.

Let's talk money, not suicide tonight.

Ar and Ego enter a subway station and board a train to Harlem -

Ar: *If I stick to your plan,*

Will you make me the man?

Ego: *With you as my fan we'll make money, and...*

I've said it before, and I'll say it again.

I hate this man. For no reason I can't stand him.

Now I need your help so we can underhand him.

It takes money to make money. Let's do it.

Put money on his downfall. I will see to it,

That your money is well spent and soon we'll invent,

A sick plan with razor sharp content.

Ar: *Where's our next meet at?*

Ego: *Right, a place to meet at?*

You know where I live.

So you know where to meet at.

Ar: *I'll be anywhere you want.*

Ego: *I can see that.*

Ar: *I'll bring you all the cash you want.*

Ego: *I believe that.*

Ego exits the train leaving Ar behind -

Aside -

Ego*: I will make a lot of money off this fool.*

I learned more in the streets than I could in school,

Once I'm in it there are no limits to what I'll do.

I can't sleep. Most nights fill my mind with hate.

While Clear, he thinks I'm loyal. Yet all that's fake.

I need to have his friendship with Cash disgraced.

Have Clear make me his ace. I got it.

Put his wife between them. When she flirts, I spot it.

Blow it out of proportion. Get Clear thinking,

That all his sweet thoughts, are somehow stinking.

He's trustworthy, and open minded.

I'll open up his nose, with my ass beside it.

Hell yes. That's all. It's on from this night.

Now, this ratchet plan can breathe life.

I'll turn his world so cold he breathes ice.

I know it sounds wrong, but it feels so right,

When darkness falls to stand my plans in the light.

Audio #12 | <u>Act 2 Scene 1A</u>

Toni, Pierce, and Hunter speak to each other in a frenzied manner between short breaks from their respective cell phone conversations. Basking in the comfort of Clear's opulent high-end loft, the three men make an array of phone calls in anticipation of his return. Clear's personal bodyguard Angel stands near the front door of the apartment, eating a large sandwich and watching videos on his phone.

The loft décor boasts a flawless blend of contemporary African art and Asian inspired furniture. Pierce sits on the sofa looking down into a coffee table shaped like a glass box, with a surface that is both a tabletop and computer screen. On the wall in front of him, a 65" curved TV sits on a thick sandstone mantel above a marble fireplace. There are four different news programs broadcasting on the screen simultaneously.

Hunter paces back and forth between the kitchen and the living room. On the second floor above the dining room, Toni stares out into the blue sky through a set of clean glass doors overlooking a two-story deck. The deck seems to float in the clouds above the city. The spacious outdoor setting is complete with a hot tub, small pool, and spectacular view of the New York city skyline. The doorbell rings and Hunter pushes the intercom button on the security monitor near the front door. Cash jokingly yells at Hunter to buzz him up to the apartment.

Hunter turns to the other men in the room with a smirk and reluctantly buzzes Cash into the building. Knowing what to expect, Hunter opens the front door, leaving it ajar to keep Cash from banging on it obnoxiously before he enters the loft. When he arrives upstairs, Cash bangs on the open door anyway. He enters the apartment in an uproar, playfully greeting everyone with a raised voice. Without looking up from his phone, he drops down onto the couch and immediately goes into a tirade about his travels.

Pierce interrupts him to point out a suspicious truck in front of the building showing up on the security monitor. Cash instructs Pierce to go down to the lobby and identify the unexpected visitors. He grabs a holstered weapon and a set of hand radios from a closet. He gives one of the radios to Pierce on his way out, along with a nickel plated 38 inside of an ankle holster. On the elevator, Pierce secures the weapon to his lower leg, prepared to confront the unknown party with force.

Cash waits patiently before speaking into the radio. He watches the security monitor and smiles after listening to Pierce's description of the mystery guests headed up to the apartment. A few minutes pass and Diamond enters the loft wearing a linen outfit with a sheer veil. She removes her sunglasses and walks over to Cash with the demeanor of a supermodel, greeting him with a kiss on the cheek.

Audio #13 | *"Homecoming"*

Toni, Angel, Pierce and Hunter sit around Clear's apartment -

Toni: *Have you heard about them,*

Coming back from overseas?

Angel: *They left from a flooded airport so we'll see.*

Toni: *With weather that bad, I wonder when they'll land.*

Call the airport and then, see where we stand.

Pierce: *Word from my contact that worked with Turk,*

Said, "His whole crew was hurt. His empire is dirt."

A dark cloud was on him. No one had time to warn him.

They flooded his Aston Martin, with a carton of shotgun shells,

And I'm assuming it's true.

Toni: *What else could we do? I'm looking at the news.*

It says a plane went down, and nobody was found.

And everybody on board burned up or drowned.

Either way we should have heard something by now.

Hunter: *Maybe they had trouble after banging the Turk out,*

Ran into the cops and they had to put that work out.

They probably had to get their passports changed,

And come back with different names on different planes.

Toni: Out of all their options, that was the very last.

Hunter: Cash just hit me with a text from the Ave,
At about quarter past. He had to catch a cab.
His plane took off first and Clear's left last.

Toni: I'm glad.

Hunter responds to a phone text -

Hunter: Hold up. Now Cash just asked,
Have we heard anything on the news,
About a plane crash?

Toni: If that's Clear's plane, we'll soon see.
Heaven only knows if he paid his final fee.
He's a soldier like me, a soldier to the D.
Now let's manage the damage,
And talk to Mike C.

Hunter: I agree. I will keep calling his cell.
And checking airport arrivals from now to 12:00 pm.
That's Cash at the door from how he's ringing the bell.
How much you want to bet he has a story to tell?

Cash bursts into the apartment -

Cash: What's the deal warriors…? I'm back in Manhattan!!!

It got messy, guns clapping cars crashing.

We almost lost it. On the flight I was strapped in.

I hope Clear gets back safe and nothing happened.

Toni: He's on a private jet?

Cash: Yes. It's a small one.

But the pilots a vet he met back in Folsom.

Angel: Just found out about our party midtown.

We got VIP spots. We should get ready now.

Cash: Hold up. Slow it down. No need to rush.

Pierce: If he's not picking up, you just have to text him.

Cash: I'll tell him where we're going, so he won't think we left him.

Pierce looks down on to the street from the apartment window -

Pierce: New truck, pulling up with nice rims.

Smoke gray tinted windows, so you can't peek in.

Dog tags on the plates, so it must be a friend.

Cash: Or a foe... Slow your roll.

Hand me the 4-4. Go down.

See who it is, and then let me know.

Pierce exits the apartment with a walkie talkie in hand -

Pierce: On the double yo.

Toni: Clear has a wife on the low?

Cash: Most definitely so, she's a pro. No question.

Everywhere she goes, flashbulbs in her direction.

She's worth nothing less than, $25 mil,

According to the New York Times and that's real.

Now, who is this stepping out the new wheels?

Pierce reports back to Cash via walkie talkie -

Pierce: Somebody named Ego. He's telling me that he goes,

Way back with Clear and he's here with his people.

Cash: News travels fast. Let him pass. He's family.

All this insanity, Diamond needed protection.

Toni: My cousin is the woman in question?

Cash: In the flesh. We left her with Ego.

His profession is weapons. Truth be told,

I thought he'd be here before I stepped in.

Cash smiles at Diamond as she enters the room -

Cash: Oh... You should be so bold. Put the world on hold.

I will let it be told. I've never seen a woman lifting ice so cold,

Look so hot. Make room in the spot, for the downtown queen,

And her brand-new rock.

Diamond: You know you need to stop that.

Tell me is my man back?

Cash: He's on his way,

But his plane didn't land yet.

Diamond: You parted ways,

But you know you didn't plan that.

Cash: Yes, we had to adjust for five-O.

O.K. that's that. It's a wrap. Now here we go.

Audio #14 | <u>**Act 2 Scene 1B**</u>

Ego starts an argument with his wife Millie. He ends up in a juvenile debate with Diamond who jumps in to defend her friend. After an extended round of verbal gymnastics, the two agree to disagree and put a stop to the discussion for the time being. Ego sarcastically tips his head toward Diamond and excuses himself.

Diamond walks away and takes a seat next to Cash on the couch. Ego turns to the mirror in the dining room to check his appearance. He looks over his shoulder past his reflection in the mirror and notices Diamond and Cash flirting innocently with each other. Through the open doors of the roof deck, the faint sound of a custom car horn travels up into the apartment.

Diamond is certain the sound of the distinct melody is from Clear's truck. She runs into the hallway, striking a sensual pose in front of the elevator doors and greets Clear when he arrives. Clear steps off the elevator and scolds her playfully. He scoops her into the air with his embrace and spins her around. Ego watches their exaggerated show of affection, trying to hide his disdain.

Audio #15 | *"Art of Words"*

Diamond snatches at Cash's phone -

Diamond: Stop playing with me.

If that's Clear, then let me know.

Cash: Give me a second to greet my people at the door.

You're looking good ma. Haven't seen you in a minute.

She's still a dime Ego. All respect intended.

Ego: For as good as she looks,

She talks just as much. In an hour from now,

You'll be screaming I've had enough.

Diamond: She hasn't said a word.

You have yet to shut up.

Ego: Have faith. It takes a minute for her to start up.

Usually when I'm hard up for sleep we get into it.

Millie: That's why they call you Ego, and you stay stuck to it.

Ego: Come on. Stop it. You know how women do it.

Line things up the way you want and run through it.

Cute when you want something. Wild when you flaunt something.

Mean as the devil, when you know you want to hurt something.

Diamond: That's just half-true.

You need to stop fronting.

Ego: No sweetie I've slept with the proof.

Women's words grow legs in the bed,

And run loose.

Millie: Humph. Keep my name out your mouth.

Ego: No doubt.

Diamond: Am I the type you're talking about?

Ego: Don't ask if you don't want what's real coming out.

Diamond: Then let's have real talk,

And not the dummy route.

Ego: You're getting serious on me,

And taking the fun out.

Diamond: When a woman's talk gets real,

You want to run out?

Ego: I light up enough real talk to put the sun out.

Argue with a hummingbird. Make him take his hum out.

Where I'm from "real talk," means pull your gun out.

A smart woman knows not to let that come out.

Diamond: What if she has a smart mouth, and can't help it?

Ego: Then she has a man that will show her how to be dealt with.

Diamond: The more you talk the worse it gets.

Millie: He hasn't even started with his foolishness yet.

Ego: If we're talking about foolishness, life's unfair.

A lot of women act real foul and still get theirs.

Diamond: Guess you've never seen men act up in the club,

 Pulling foolish women, that show no love.

Ego: Yes, that's exactly the type that I'm speaking of,

But... good women still put you through,

The same type of foolishness the foul one's do.

Diamond: I really hate to say it but you're ignorant as hell,

If you can't tell the difference between a Jezebel,

And a woman with her head on straight.

Ego: In that case; you really think I'm just an ignorant ape.

Listen up, while I quote Shakespeare the great.

"She that was ever fair and never proud,

Had tongue at will and yet was never loud,

Never lacked gold and yet went never gay,

Fled from her wish and yet said, "Now I may,"

She at being angered, her revenge being nigh,

Bade her wrong stay and her displeasure fly,

She that in wisdom never was so frail,

To change the cod's-head for the salmon's tail;

She that could think and ne'er disclose her mind,

See suitors following and not look behind,

She was a wit, if ever such wits were.-"

Diamond: To do what?

Ego: Give birth at two kids per,

And advertise beer, bikinis and mink fur.

Diamond: You really are a lame. Your conclusions are faulty.

Here's a quote for you. "Little tic, get off me."

Cash: You know how it is where he from. Candid and crossly.
In situations with bullets flying cross me, I can't trade him,
Being un-PC, for the toughest Harvard teacher, with a PhD.

Aside -

Ego: I see. Whisper. Kiss her palm. Tickle her on her arm.
He's so cool and calm. Mr. Fly Mike Cash-ass headed for a web,
That was spun for a dummy. He's got nothing on me.
This is a web designed to catch big money.

Ego: It sounds like your boy is back.

Cash: It's got to be.

Diamond: I'm the first person that he's going to want to see.

Cash: I was given orders not to let you leave.

Diamond: And who's going to stop me? Come on, Cash please.

Clear enters the room and grabs Diamond playfully -

Clear: You know this is not where you're supposed to be.

Diamond: Excuse me. I'm sorry. Are you talking to me?
Are you the one that they call, "Clear" around here?

Clear: *Are you the reason there's no fear around here?*

The reason I would fly my Lear through rough weather,

And go through whatever just to bring us back together.

Aside -

Ego: *He couldn't feel fresher. He's feeling no pressure,*

Smoother than a top ten billboard record.

I will bring him down a peg, just for sheer pleasure.

And honestly when it's done, I'll feel much better.

Audio #16 | **Act 2 Scene 1C**

Clear throws a set of keys to Ego who catches them ineptly against his chest. He shares a few words with his guests before he and Diamond enter their bedroom to prepare for the night's festivities at her nightclub. Ego discreetly walks out onto the deck and calls down to the lobby on the house phone. The building attendant at the front desk answers Ego's call. Ar has spent the last hour waiting in the lobby for Ego to call him about the party.

The attendant confirms Ego as the caller and hands the receiver to Ar. Up in the apartment, Ego sits on the roof deck alone. He speaks to Ar over the phone with his voice just above a whisper. They briefly discuss their intentions to use Cash's presence during the evening's celebration to create a rift between Clear and Diamond. Ego shares some detailed instructions with Ar and hangs up. After Ego ends the call, Ar hands the phone receiver back to the attendant, thanks him with a tip and leaves the building.

Audio #17 | "Still Shady"

Clear and Diamond head to their bedroom as Ego makes a call -

Clear: From here on out let's put aside all hassles. We have VIP spots,

Waiting at Club Castle. Toni I will get at you later to catch us up.

Take the keys to the Bentley. Ego have it pulled up. For the next month,

The paparazzi is playing rough. We'll go in through the back of the club,

To ease it up. Tonight the wife and I will look so tough,

The flashes on the cannons can't help but to bust.

To Ar over the phone -

Ego: Make sure the valet has the car scrubbed, and get to the club,

Before security does. I hate to say it, but that girl is in love.

Ar: Now that sounds bugged.

Ego: I know it does but... It's a want to be seen with a thug,

That type of love. He keeps talking money and she gets fed up.

The next thing you know, she's calling the F.E.D.S. up.

When he figures it all out, then the bubble will bust.

Their feelings won't be as tight as federal handcuffs.

Really what she's feeling is lust, that will be dust.

This illusion she's holding up, that will be crushed.

Then thinking of his sperm in her will feel like venom.

His big empty shoes, Mike Cash will want to fill them.

Diamond has that look. She wants to get with him.

Ar: No, that can't be. She's not that simple.

Ego exits the apartment and heads toward the elevator -

Ego: Behind those dimples, there's a bad girl in her.

I caught her with her lips up close to the sinner.

But tonight, I'll put you on top like a winner.

And you'll rule like Slick Rick from here to Venice.

This is where we play Cash like Wimbledon tennis.

Watch for my command, when you see me from afar.

I doubt Cash knows who you are, so play the star.

Front hard on him and order the caviar. Buy out the bar.

Bump into him. Draw a crowd to him.

Make sure that he's drunk first.

Get him to the point where he thinks,

Maybe you'll dump first.

Ar: Then what?

Ego: He'll probably want to put you in black hearse.

Throw him off until he's only thinking to blast first.

Make him seem tasteless. Get him out of sorts.

Play him like a sport. Make judgment an afterthought.

He'll act rash. Then his betters will cut him short.

Teach him a costly lesson. That's when you'll step in.

You'll go from being nobody to street legend.

Ar: *Not to second guess you, but answer this question.*

How will I get into the VIP section?

Ego: *My connection at Hotel Citadel,*

Right across from Castle, owes me blessing.

He's a recognized VIP on every guest list.

He'll give me the tickets. I hand them off to you.

Ar: *I'll meet you at the hotel, between 12:00 am and 2:00 am.*

Ego hangs up with Ar and exits the apartment building -

Aside -

Ego: *Cash and Diamond are much like brother and sis.*

I won't quit, until it makes Clear flip, into felony jealousy,

Turned domestic violence, thoughts of aggravated assault

That can't be silenced. But... keep Ar in the mix,

Right at the hip until Cash starts to slip,

Off the edge. Let Clear push him off the ledge.

It's been said, Mike had my wife in bed.

So in my mind, he's already off and dead.

As for Clear, he'll be lost and confused,

Washed up and used, heart totally bruised,

Falling into dead end moves with no clues,

Till every choice he has left is lose-lose,

And the rest of his future is yesterday's news.

Audio #18 | <u>Act 2 Scene 2</u>

Ego ends his short call with Ar on the roof deck and heads back indoors. He returns the phone to its base and without being noticed, exits the apartment. Deciding to take the stairs instead of the elevator, he uses the empty stairwell to think out loud about his plans with Ar. He stops to steady himself at the bottom floor, acknowledging the end of his long descent with a hefty sigh.

Leaning against the wall on the last step, Ego pauses for a moment before opening the door to the lobby. On his way out of the building, he hands the doorman the keys to Clear's Rolls Royce. He dismissively orders for the vehicle to be cleaned, prepped and ready to travel within the hour. Once outside, he rushes across the pavement and squeezes between two parked cars. Determined to get to the club before Clear's entourage, he stands with his arm raised at the edge of traffic and flags down a cab.

When he finally settles into the back seat, Ego is momentarily caught off guard by images of Clear and Diamond on the screen in front of him. He turns up the volume on the tiny monitor. An entertainment reporter commences with a news story about Clear and Diamond, labeling them New York's hottest couple. Before signing off, the reporter goes on to advertise their upcoming party at Diamond's Club Castle, where all of the city's leading music artists are headed to celebrate with them for the evening.

Audio #19 | *"NUZEE Luv Ballad"*

Entertainment news blares from a car radio on the street -

Reporter: *Who's the sexiest New York knight?*

Who brings pleasure to the New York night?

Well Clear the air. Girl I know that's right.

No need for excess light. He's got a Diamond,

5'9, a full figure and straight shining.

You know they hit the hottest spots on the islands,

From that new club Bonfire in the Bahamas,

To right here in Manhattan, now bring the comma,

You can't stand it. Well, have a seat! Here comes the drama.

We get it first at N.U.Z. double E.

Our sources say they're about to get married.

You can see the royal couple tonight at Club Castle.

A big night, in the Big Apple, don't let it pass you.

Come as you are, or dress like a star.

Order the caviar. Drink from the open bar.

The party won't end until 5:00 am tomorrow.

Hosted by Cyprus, old school, Kid Capri.

It's the party of the year for Clear, so come see.

I'm Erica Herald. So true, that's me. 100% N.U.Z. double E...

Audio #20 | <u>Act 2 Scene 3A</u>

Hours after being reunited, Diamond and Clear sit in the VIP section of her nightclub, perched above a crowded dance floor. Clear whispers something to Diamond in her ear and motions for her to leave with him. He rises from his seat, extends his hand to Cash, and offers his goodbyes. The two men shake hands at the chest and share a genuine farewell hug. Clear and Diamond exit the VIP section through a set of velvet curtains. Cash looks across the club and finishes what is left of his drink.

He makes a halfhearted attempt to get the attention of a passing barmaid for a final round. Unsuccessful in his effort to purchase one last drink, he sits his empty glass down and turns to leave. Before he can make it to the curtains of the VIP exit, Ego approaches him. Joyfully, Ego clamps his arm over Cash's shoulder and turns him back toward the dance floor. He then moves aside, providing Cash with a direct view of six beautiful young women seated down at the bar below. Ego explains to Cash that the women have invited him to join them for a drink. Cash accepts the invitation from the women and ends up drinking more than he intended.

A bartender shouts out, "last call." Diamond's cousin Toni approaches the bar to join the group for a final round of shots. After having one too many drinks, Cash stumbles to his feet and steps away from the bar. The rest of the group pay their tabs and make their exit behind him. They all end up standing outside the nightclub. The late hour has done nothing to dull the vibrant nature of the city.

Pockets of people stand together in conversation near the club entrance. Some are hailing cabs, some are using their phones to secure a ride, while others wait for a parking attendant to retrieve their car. A club valet approaches Cash to verify his parking stub. Cash drunkenly stuffs his ticket into the valet's open hand and pulls an extra set of car keys from his jacket. He walks off toward the nearby parking garage dangling his keys in the air.

Ar exits the club behind Ego and the others. He tries desperately to go unnoticed by Toni and his friends. He moves along the sidewalk uneasily, trying to get close to Ego. For a second, Toni is distracted by the sweet smile of a young woman leaving the club. Seizing on Toni's inattentiveness, Ego hisses a few words at Ar in a perturbed whisper. Ar nods and walks away as oddly as he arrived.

Audio #21 | *"Club Castle"*

Clear and Cash stand in the VIP section of a night club -

Clear: Mike C. Man, I've got to get going. The night is yours.

Don't let the liquor get you to crawling on all fours,

Banging on all doors of the girls you adore;

Or in a tussle with the first cat, that calls for it.

I'll be back to shut the club down around 4:00 am.

Cash: Ego is my ace in the hole so fall back.

When it comes to holding my liquor, I'm all that.

Clear: Yes, enough respect for E to the Gezee.

Cash: Speak of the devil, if it isn't "Young Easy."

Even though the party is hot, we have to be breezy.

Ego: With the clock barely hitting quarter past 10:00 pm.

Let men be men. You see how Clear did it. You know Diamond said,

"Let's hit it." So he can hit it.

Cash: Yeah. She's so exquisite, I would probably do the same.

Ego: She looks sweet, but I bet her games, "Got game."

Cash: A sweet mouth with sweet aim for fresh talk.

Ego: A slick eye for men who have fresh thoughts.

Cash: Maybe kind of flirty but loyal like a boss.

Ego: Well, she knows disloyalty comes with a cost.

Cash: Still, she can't be bought, not like most women.

Ego: Well, here's to Clear and Diamond swimming in linen.

Cash: No, I drank enough already to shut it down.

Ego: You think the future holds a better party than now.

Cash: Another round, and I'm a clown, time to bounce.

Ego: And leave me here, with these shots, and six chicks?

Cash: Six dimes, or six cents, stalking the click?

Ego: Six quarters down by the bar, licking their lips.

Cash: One, last round… Then we split. That will be it.

Aside -

Ego: *One shot, two shots, three shots... four.*

A fifth shot will blow the hinges of the door.

Diamond's friend Cyprus and cousins are in the building.

Normally these tough guys, wouldn't be willing,

To lift t a finger over some intoxicated club talk.

This night, I'll get Cash to make his gun talk.

For a silly reason, make him look like a heathen.

Shots of Patron will be the only thing he's breathing.

Cash: *Am I as drunk as I look? I'm off the hook.*

I'm off the books. I'm off the wagon for sure.

Toni: *I'll man up for one more with you, then hit the door.*

Ego: *You know what you need to do?*

Ego hands out drinks and sings along to the club music -

Ego: *"Blame it on the goose, feeling loose.*

Blame it on Patron. You're in a zone."

Cash: *That's that old club banger. I keep that bumping.*

Ego: *The first time I heard it, I was over in London.*

In Europe, anytime to drink is the right time.

Cash: *That's why Old English will have you out of your mind.*

Toni: *I see you're trying to get tore down, well let's do it.*

Ego: *Now that's what I'm talking about. Pass the fluids like...*

Ego and Cash drunkenly sing like Busta Rhymes -

Ego / Cash: *"Busta, see the girl rolling... And it look like."*

Ego: *Another song for the alkies. I'll get Kid to play it again.*

Cash: *No, not now E. I'm smashed to the core of my soul. Time to fold.*

Ego: *Too cold lieutenant. I see you need a minute.*

Cash stumbles to his feet as he attempts to put on his coat -

Cash: *All I need is the valet to pull up my Infinite.*

I got the semi out in the trunk, ready to pop something,

Sig Sauer in the glove box, ready to drop something.

One for my left hand and one for my right.

I'll bust shots at whoever come with it tonight.

I can walk. I can talk. I can see where I'm going.

I don't fall off because the drinks start flowing.

Pierce: *Yes, I think we all know where this is going.*

Cash: Right, you don't want to see them things start blowing.

Toni: Sure Cash, everybody knows that you're holding.

Ego: The man that you saw before doesn't exist.
When he's sober, he's a soldier like Caesar. "God's gift."

Toni: How often does he get like this? What did I miss?

Ego: Like most men sleep. Every night. That's about right.

Toni: Somebody needs to speak to Clear, about this here.

Ego whispers something to Ar as he passes him and Toni -

Ego: Ar, where you been all night? The time is near.

Toni: Anyway, what was I saying about your boy?
Oh yeah, this game is not at all for the coy,
Or men with loud mouths that make a lot of noise.

Ego: I will have to leave that alone. That's all you Tone.
I love Cash, but he's prone to be two toned.

Audio #22 | <u>Act 2 Scene 3B</u>

Gun shots ring out a short distance away from the nightclub entrance. The crowd of patrons in front of the building scatter into the street. Ego and Toni fall back into the doorway of the club. Eventually, they see Ar and Cash running toward them. Both Cash and Ar come to a stop on the red carpet in front of the club entrance. Holding a 9mm handgun with an extended clip, Cash walks angrily toward Ar. Ignoring all around him, he points his gun at Ar and slowly closes the distance between them. When the two are finally face to face, Cash's weapon is just shy of touching Ar's chest.

Cash raises the gun and fires another flurry of shots into the air. The bullets tear through the club awning and some shattered glass debris falls onto the carpet. Toni gently puts his hand on Cash's arm. Incensed by Toni's interference, Cash loses sight of his conflict with Ar and turns his misguided anger toward Toni. After a short face off, Cash and Toni exchange blows and the gun accidentally discharges, leaving Toni wounded.

Ego instructs Ar to make a scene. Following Ego's instructions Ar runs out into the street crying for help. As if summoned by Ar's shouting, Clear pulls up to the club and explodes out of his car. He leaps from behind the vehicle's rising kamikaze door and snatches Cash's weapon. Ar identifies Cash as the person responsible for the violence occurring in front of the club and runs off. With the help of one of the bouncers, Ego pulls Toni to his feet.

The small group of men file back into the club's entrance and make their way to a private office behind one of the bars. The bouncer and Ego lay Toni down on a sofa. Enraged, Clear takes a seat at his desk in the room. The cops arrive as Ego is closing the office doors. Before retreating into the room with the others, he quietly instructs the bouncer to get rid of the police. Ego closes the doors, and the men begin to recall for Clear what led to the senseless violence. Ego confirms Ar's assertion that Cash instigated the unfortunate events. Diamond enters the room and everyone except for Clear freezes up.

Clear's private doctor enters the office behind her looking for the wounded Toni. Clear gets up. He approaches Diamond to keep her from letting the door close and calmly turns her around. With the door blocking her view, she does not notice Toni writhing in pain on the couch behind her. Clear places Diamond's arm under his and nonchalantly guides her back out of the office. Everyone exits the room behind Clear and Diamond except for the doctor and Toni.

Ego and Cash trail behind the group and stop short of exiting the club. Cash's feelings are hurt, and Ego attempts to console him. The once lively party space is now a large vacant room. The empty dance floor is marred with used wine glasses, beer bottles, and party favors. Ego and Cash exit the club and part ways. The parking attendant pulls up in Cash's car. Ego watches Cash leave before calling Ar on his cell phone. He is now the only person left standing alone in front of the deserted club.

Audio #23 | "War Party"

Cash threatens Ar outside the entrance of a night club -

Cash: Yes. Get ready for these bullets to go through your chest.

Go ahead and take your last breath.

Toni moves to separate Cash and Ar -

Toni: Let's not do that here.

Come on. Stop that.

Cash: Not right now Tone.

I'll lay this whole block flat.

Ar: Go ahead and do it.

Cash: What? You mean pop that?

Toni: Listen Cash. This is for real. You need to drop that.

Cash accidently fires his weapon wounding Toni -

Cash: You can get some of this too. I'll blow your top back.

I'll leave nothing above your shoulders for a top hat,

Left to sit on... Now take your hands off me!!!

Toni: You should recognize that you don't out boss me.

I'll chalk it up to all that syrup in your cup.

Ego steps over to whisper something again to Ar -

Ego: *Ar, you need to make that move, and stir this up.*

Ar jumps out into the street yelling to the crowd-

Ar: *Can somebody stop this, want to be John Gotti,*

From catching a body, right in front of the spot?

Clear pulls up to the building and jumps from his vehicle -

Clear: *The last thing I need right now,*

Is to get hot.

Toni: *The last thing I needed from Cash, was to get shot.*

But believe it or not, I'm on the block leaking.

You picked the wrong side of the pool.

This is the deep end.

Ego: *Cut short all the talk of getting even.*

Clear and the men head to a room back inside the club -

Clear: *I will cut all of you short of even breathing.*

You think I'm taking this lightly. Try me slightly.

I put souls in a hole, where it's likely, you'll never be found.

You know how I get down. Tell Kid I said cut it.

The party is over now. It's a thin line between love,

And my wrath. Do I have to ask how did we get on this path?

Ego: *Tell the truth really, the answer is kind of gray.*

Model chicks out by the bar... What can I say?

Next thing you know guns out,

Ready to slay.

Clear: *Put your money where your mouth is.*

Cash, you seem to be quiet about this.

Cash: *I did enough already,*

I'm staying out of this.

Clear: *Toni, what's the story?*

Let's talk about this.

Toni: *I wish I could, but I can't. It's too much.*

If I pass out on this couch, I won't get up.

I can barely sit up. I'm about to spit up.

With this hole in my gut,

Every second's pressing my luck.

Ego saw everything happen up to the end.

Clear: *On everything in heaven,*

My patience is getting thin.

I'm all ears Ego, please do begin.

Toni: *Speak anything untrue, that's on you.*

The streets will remember what weak men do.

Ego: *Who knew?*

Who thought things would come down to,

My low comfort level with the snitch position.

We got outside and Mike Cash started flipping.

Gunplay displayed on some dude from the party.

Tone steps in. He's like, "Take it down a notch."

They locked horns and then the gun, "goes pop."

Clear: *That was easy enough, and this is hard but,*

I will have to cut Mike Cash short of my trust.

Diamond enters the room followed by an EMT -

Diamond: *Clear what's the problem here?*

Clear: *Problem solved. A small mix up at the club but it's resolved.*

Cash and Ego stay behind as the others exit with the EMT -

Ego: *Was it something I said, that hurt your feelings C.?*

Cash: *Forget feelings B. Pride is killing me.*

Ego: *God forgives... Let time do the healing G.*

Cash: Once a rep is lost, nothing can heal it E.
You put the knife in my back, but unwillingly.

Ego: Clear can't stay pissed, not over this.
He needs you like he needs five fingers to make a fist.

Cash: Soon as he turns his back, I'm swigging a fifth,
Of Hennie and sends me right into the mosh pit.
It would be different dog... if this was an "off night."
But I was off tonight. That's on me!!!
I know you have love for me Ego but let it be.

Ego: Who hasn't had a night, where they had a little too much?
How many haters have tried to split us up like a Dutch?

Cash: Let the liquor tell it tonight, they might have succeeded.

Ego: This is not the Cash I know, talking defeated.
The writings on the wall, written for you to read it.
Take this lesson and heed it. Capture the beast and feed it.
Let Diamond be the one to decide how you should be treated.

Cash: It sounds like a good plan. What's first to precede it?

Ego: Words from the heart, where that love is deep seeded.

Cash: *I see it, and believe it. I'll catch her, at the gym.*

Ego: *That's right. Make amends. Good night. I'm turning in.*

Cash exits -

Cash: *True. I chuck the deuce up, until we meet again.*

Aside -

Ego: *How can anybody say that I'm a bad guy? Honest, I never lie.*

Cash wants to be, Clear's monkey again, his flunky again.

Who am I to say he shouldn't try? And why not talk to Diamond,

When she's easy on the eyes? Frame like an hourglass,

They can't let an hour pass, without getting flirty

And that's my fault? Why? Maybe that makes Clear jealous.

Oh my. Maybe Cash gets overzealous. He's so fly.

I'm just trying to help him out. All can go to hell about,

Whether this thing goes south. Don't make me cry.

The more Cash pushes the matter to Diamond

And Diamond pushes the matter to Clear,

The madder Clear gets. I'll put a little bug in his ear.

Turn his love into fear, so when she starts talking Cash,

He gets upset. By then I'm out of it like, gross to net profit.

Once they're at each other's throat...

Who am I to stop it?

Ego answers a phone call from Ar -

Ego: Where're you at son?

You did your job quite nicely.

Ar: Every little thing with you, has been about what might be.

Now I'm having doubts. The bottom is falling out.

Did I mention how I almost got my brains blown out!!!

Ego: Chill. Wait a second. Hold up. Calm down!!!

Everything you want is almost right inside your palm now.

Cash put a gun in your face. Pull your skirt up.

Take a pill. Take a nap. Don't be soft. Call an escort service.

Get a chick up in your loft. I'm off!!!

Ego ends the call -

Aside -

Ego: I still need something for my plan,

Maybe I should put some rumors out on Instagram.

I'm close to a winner, but cold as the winter.

A cold day in hell, is a holiday for a sinner.

Time is like a gambler's money. It gets thinner.

This plot's a Russian roulette gun.

Watch how I spin her.

Audio #24 | **Act 3 Scene 1**

It is a partly sunny morning. Intermittent sun showers fall from a few scattered clouds hanging above midtown Manhattan. Cash parks his motorcycle in front of a private social club. He dismounts the bike, lowers the kickstand, and sits sideways atop the leather seat. His uncharacteristically disheveled appearance marks his lack of sleep since his altercation with Toni a few hours ago. He comforts himself with a hot cup of coffee, taking a small amount of pleasure in watching members come and go from the gym inside. He tries desperately to fight through the throbbing in his head from an enormous hangover. His efforts to manage the pounding headache are thwarted by the sounds of the city as it awakens.

A few doors down from where he sits two street performers sing, dance, and drum out a succession of the latest popular songs. Using instruments fashioned from household items including a drum set made of buckets and wooden spoons they are incessantly loud. Their drumming and singing are devastating to Cash's condition at the moment. He approaches the two men and asks them to move on. He casually lifts up his shirt, revealing a handgun tucked into his belt. Cash grabs the dancing street performer by the arm before he can run off. He turns him around and drags him back toward the private club. Cash receives a call from Ego on his cell phone. With the street performer's arm still in his grasp, he asks Ego to hold on for a minute. He releases the man only after ordering him to go into the club and find his friend Diamond.

Looking at his reflection in the window of a parked car, the dancer straightens his clothes and pats down his hair. He turns around flamboyantly and dances up the steps into the building. Cash returns to his conversation with Ego while waiting for the man to return. Moments later, Millie comes out of the building behind the street dancer. He walks over to Cash with his hand out. Cash lifts his shirt again, showing his gun. The dancer performs an improvised pop-locking shuffle and scurries off. Cash ends his call with Ego and greets Millie with a kiss on the cheek.

Audio #25 | *"Jealous Never Worry"*

Cash parks his motorcycle near a private membership club -

Cash: Yo, son. I'll give you a yard,

If you would stop beating that drum,

Beat it like MJ and take your drums with you.

Dancer: Yo, son. If I were you, with a bike like that,

And you were me, with these skills. See how I bounce like that?

You wouldn't catch me trying to knock your hustle down like that.

Drummer: That's right. We're out here grinding.

What's the real issue?

Dancer: Awe he's hung over. Poor baby needs a tissue.

Drummer: If you gave us two yards,

We'll leave but then we'll miss you.

Dancer: But make it five and we'll be out of here like a missile.

Drummer: For a grand, we could get married,

And fall in love with you.

Dancer: Or you and your hangover could... hang out with us.

We do train platforms, sidewalks, even the bus.

Drummer: Or you can let the lead bust, Mr. Tough Guy.

Cash lifts his shirt revealing a weapon tucked at his side -

Dancer: Oops, I had something in my eye. I didn't see that.

Look at the time. I have somewhere else I should be at.

Drummer: So true. I have to move. I have to go. Time flies.

I'mma let you two hug it out on your own and say goodbye.

Dancer: Yes. Peace. Be out. What the hell were you thinking?

Can't you see the man's had a long night of heavy drinking?

Cash grabs one of the men as they try and hurry off -

Cash: Before you go, answer me this, and make it quick.

I have a lady friend that goes to this gym.

Seen her go in?

Dancer: Oh yeah, again and again,

The one who takes the spin class?

Cash: Funny, but not funny enough to duck a pimp smack.

So what you need to do is go inside and check for a,

Girl named Diamond with diamonds dripping like ice water,

Over her ring finger. Maybe you'll get a quarter.

Cash receives a call from Ego and gestures for the man to leave -

Ego: Still haven't been home yet?

Cash: Nothing to bone yet. Still haven't got in the habit of,
Sleeping alone yet. That's another topic. Have you talked to Millie?

Ego: They're at the gym together, we're swinging by to get her.
You better catch her now if you want to speak with her.

Cash ends his call as Milli walks up after tipping the man -

Millie: Good morning love. I heard about what happened at the club.
You need to come inside, see this masseuse, and get your back rubbed.
Clear told Diamond, "I'm not messing with that dude no more."
Yeah right, I bet he will call you tonight.

Cash: You might be right, but do me a favor all right.
Tell Diamond we need to talk. I know her time is tight.

Millie: Come and tell her yourself. She's finishing her workout.
Say what you have to say. Everything will work out.

Cash: If it does, then you know it's not a surprise,
You'll get a day trip to the spa and the whole nine.

Audio #26 | **Act 3 Scene 2**

Followed by another vehicle, Clear pulls up to Ego's apartment in Harlem. His block is filled with newly renovated homes. From his front door, Ego acknowledges Clear with a wave and ends the phone conversation he is having with Mike Cash. Wearing an Adidas track suit and running shoes, he trots down his front steps, jogs up to the lead car and jumps into the front seat next to Clear. Ego curiously scans the interior of the vehicle and spots a bag filled with money on the floor of the back seat. He reaches back and pulls the bag up from the floor. He puts it in his lap and flips through some of the bills. Clear shares some information about the purpose of the money and the two vehicles pull off into traffic.

Audio #27 | *"Worry Less"*

Clear and Ego drive through the streets of New York -

Clear: *Make sure these stacks get back to the boss.*

Tell him nothing is off. We're still putting that work in.

Ego: *Anything else?*

Clear: *No, I feel certain. Big money speaks for itself.*

Ego: *Let's do some dirt then.*

Audio #28 | **Act 3 Scene 3A**

Cash and Millie greet Diamond outside the entrance of the social club after her workout. She is expecting to meet briefly with Clear in front of the building before she leaves. He is on his way to use the private gun range located in the basement of the facility. Still breathing heavily from her exercise routine, small traces of sweat glisten over Diamond's strikingly smooth skin. She and Millie converse with Cash on the sidewalk until they notice Clear's vehicle approaching in the distance. Cash extends a rushed goodbye to Diamond and jumps on his motorcycle. He peels off before Clear's small convoy can make the light at the corner. Clear arrives just as Cash is pulling out. He parks and watches Cash speed away on his bike as he exits his car. He is dressed in a Nike sweatsuit and a pair of Air Jordans. Diamond embraces him with a big hug.

Clear's bodyguard Angel exits the second vehicle and pays for parking. Angel puts a parking receipt on the dashboard of the truck he was driving. He then walks over and climbs in behind the wheel of the car Clear was leading in. Millie grabs their gym bags and gets in the backseat of the car behind Angel. Clear opens the back door for Diamond on the passenger side. He gives her a kiss on the neck as she sinks down into the seat next to Millie. They share a few words and the car pulls off. Clear walks back to the truck Angel was driving. He grabs a bag from the rear cab of the vehicle. He closes and locks the doors of the truck then walks into the building with Ego. Everyone greets Clear warmly as he walks by. Clear and Ego walk toward a set of elevators to go down to the gun range.

Audio #29 | *"The Big Approach"*

Cash greets Diamond as she approaches his motorcycle -

Diamond: Cash, I'm glad to see you.

You don't have to explain to us.

Millie: We believe you. With us nothing has changed.

Ego is feeling the pain like it's his fault.

Diamond: But it's not. No one needs to take this loss.

You're Clear's brother in arms, when Duke rings the alarm

And it's time to bomb, keep calm and carry on.

You're waiting for a call? Well, you won't be waiting long.

Cash: You're holding me down strong. I will owe you forever.

Diamond: I will have you back together, tougher than leather.

Cash: If so, you have to be clever.

From here on in, it might be like,

"Oh yeah Cash, remember him?"

Diamond: No, I doubt that. You'll get your clout back.

Ask Millie. Clear gets open like the outback,

When I perform for him, the things that I perform.

Old school De La, to the break of dawn.

Millie sees Clear's car approaching -

Millie: *You should hit the cut.*

That's him about to pull up.

Cash: *Yup, that's his truck. That's that. My time is up.*

Diamond: *Let me talk to him real fast.*

Let's see what's up.

Cash: *I'd rather not press my luck. I'll chalk it up.*

Diamond: *If you insist.*

Ego points out Cash as he pulls off on his motorcycle -

Ego: *Oh my God. What's this?*

Clear: *What's what?*

Ego: *Oh, just another nut pushing up.*

Clear: *That's Cash looking for Diamond, to give him a pass.*

Ego: *No, if that was him, he wouldn't take off so fast.*

Clear: *He knows if we come too close, we're bound to clash.*

Diamond greets Clear cheerfully as he exits his car -

Diamond: *Hey sweetie... Did you see me and your boy Cash?*

I already know. I won't ask. You're still mad.

Clear: *Why did he leave so fast? Tell me that.*

Diamond: *Because when you're mad at people,*

You don't know how to act.

Clear: *All right. Whatever.*

Let's talk about something else.

Diamond: *You know I'll bring it up again.*

I'm just trying to help.

Clear: *Not right now, so dead it and let it go.*

Diamond: *Whenever you're ready to talk about it let me know.*

Clear: *Let's put this on hold. I got things to do.*

Diamond: *Can we talk over dinner?*

Clear: *No, I'm with the crew.*

Diamond: How about tomorrow night or Tuesday when you're home?

Or when we get a break, we can talk it through, on the phone.

You know how I feel about it, I won't leave it alone.

When we were off and on, and I was on my own,

Cash was the only one saying not to move on.

Clear: No promises made. Give me some time to think on it.

Diamond: Do me a favor. Think fast and think Cash.

That's what you were getting when you were tight on the Ave.

For real. In the end, he's your friend and I fear,

Over one bad night you'll lose a lot of good years.

Clear: I said I'd think about it.

Diamond gets in the car preparing to drive off -

Diamond: Huh, I don't doubt it, but don't talk or think about it.

Be about it, and when you're ready for this love,

Come and see about it.

Clear: I'll need that in about an hour.

I'm a beast without it.

Audio #30 | **Act 3 Scene 3B**

Clear approaches a set of elevator doors and swipes a badge to call the elevator. The sign next to the doors reads, "Gun Range - Ground Floor." Clear and Ego take the elevator down. They sign some papers at a desk in the hallway on the ground floor and enter the locker room behind it. Once in the locker room, Ego shares with Clear his suspicions of Diamond. They each find their locker and remove a handgun case. They inspect their weapons and close up the lockers before leaving the room. A bit bothered by the choice of topic, Clear subtly grabs Ego by the collar.

Clear smiles devilishly as he pushes Ego against the wall. He expresses his concern with Ego's insinuations about Diamond and Cash with a few harsh words. He then slowly loosens his grip on Ego and menacingly steps back a few inches. He smiles again, pats Ego on the shoulder and walks away still aggravated with his friend, but content to hear him out for a little bit longer. They walk into the firing range down the hall. They place their gun cases on a steel table in the room and open them.

Each man removes from his case a handgun, shooting glasses and ear covers. They load their weapons and step into their firing booths. Clear takes aim at his target and begins shooting. Ego carries on with his disturbing insights and both men stop periodically to talk between firing rounds. Weary of Ego's dark notions, Clear takes off his ear covers and coolly removes his shooting glasses. He pulls the slide back on his weapon, puts a single bullet in the chamber and walks over to Ego's firing both.

Ego removes his protective gear and unloads his weapon, placing everything in front of him. He begins to cautiously temper his words. Reassured by the change in Ego's approach to their conversation, Clear returns to his firing booth. He reloads his weapon with a full clip, takes aim at his target and squeezes off a few rounds in rapid succession. Ego follows Clear to his booth and speaks almost directly in his ear.

Clear reloads his weapon again with Ego hovering sinisterly over his shoulder. He aims at his target and listens until Ego has definitively raised his suspicions about Diamond and Cash. Ego prepares to leave. He checks his weapon and returns it to the gun case with the rest of his safety gear. Finally, Ego exits the room and Clear waits for the door to close before firing another rapid series of shots at his target.

With the clip empty he slams the weapon down in front of him. The range falls silent and he begins talking through his thoughts out loud. Clear's cell phone rings. He looks at the phone on the table in front of him and sees it is Diamond calling. He gathers his firearm along with the rest of his shooting equipment and places them back in the gun case. He declines the call and slams the door on his way out of the range.

Audio #31 | *"Thin Air"*

Ego and Clear enter the private members club together -

Clear: Even though I love her to death,

If I ever had a reason to hate her,

As much as I love her, I would be a mess.

Ego: Little girls will play.

Clear: Wait, what did you say?

Ego: Did Cash know about your relationship,

From the first day?

Clear: He was the first and the last.

What's the reason you ask?

Ego: You know your boy Cash.

Clear: I do. What are you saying?

Ego: Nothing. Not a thing.

But they go back like that?

Clear: Way back, like that.

Ego: Honestly, like that?

Clear: Like what, like that?

What do you mean by that?

Ego: I don't know, just that.

Clear: Just what, just that?

Ego: I don't think it's like that.

Clear: You don't think it's like what?

I say, "What's that?" And then you echo me back.

"Like that, like that." And now I'm like, "What's that?"

In the corner of your mind, off to the side, in the back,

Like the barrel of a semi-auto mac about to bust back,

Then you see Cash and say,

"It's nothing like that."

Ego: Well in fact, I love you like a lyric loves music.

Clear: Do you? Then say what's in your head

Before I lose it. Or you lose yours. Choose one, either | or...

Either way, you could end up with your brains all over this floor.

Then I'll know what's on your mind once I'm standing on it.

Ego: Then let me man up on it and say Cash is a hustler.

Clear: And?

Ego: He plays his part with all that he could muster.

Clear: If he didn't, he would be a buster with a gun.

Ego: You know what you're exactly right, the thought I had was dumb.

Clear: If it's messy, leave a mess. No need for flinching.

Ego: Listen, not that I'm snitching. You know I'm not a snitch.
That type of talk leaves deep wounds no one can stitch.

Cash: You got a beef with the kid? Must be something I missed.

Ego: No beefs, no riffs. The streets are talking a bit.

Clear: Dog! You're making me sick. Say what you're saying!

Ego: Put it this way. You're either serious or playing.
And sometimes when you're playing things can get serious.
Cats can go from laughing, to pulling out four fifths
And just as quick, say something slick and back to talking trash.

Clear: I swear, keep talking in circles,

And it will get bad.

Ego: I'd rather have you mad at me,

Then say what's on my mind.

Clear: My patience is getting thin.

This feels like a waste of time.

Ego: I'll simply say be careful.

A jealous man is blind.

Preoccupied with trying to find out,

Things he shouldn't find.

Clear and Ego take an elevator down to an indoor gun range -

Clear: That's where I draw the line.

Ego: From a baller to crime. No matter what,

There'll be somebody trying to steal your shine.

Clear: No one is taking mine. I'm on top of my grind.

I got the hottest wife in the city. I let her speak her mind.

Keep up with the times, wearing the finest vines,

Good head on her shoulders, strong will, strong spine.

Ego: You're a bigger man than me. You've got the spirit of a lion.
Love, louder than his roar. I still think something's off,
With your woman, but to be sure. If I were you,
I'd open up my eyes a little more. Sunday holy and pure,
Monday kisses galore, Tuesday she's out the door, Wednesday,
You're in court. She's taking half of everything and more.

Clear: And you think Diamond is like that at her core?

Ego: She played her father out for you, and seemed to feel secure.

Clear: That's real talk.

Ego: That's why you need to play the hawk. I know you love her.
I'm telling you all this as your brother.

Clear and Ego load handguns and start shooting at targets -

Clear: I know you got me covered.

Ego: But I'm bringing you down.

Clear: No, keep shooting rounds.
.

Ego: Sorry for how it sounds.

Clear: *You tend to be up front. Don't front.*

Ego: *We're just talking, but I see your shoulders getting hunched.*

Clear: *I'm good son. I know my woman has always been true.*

Ego: *Yes. Maybe to you, and it should stay that way.*

Clear: *It comes so natural to women, all the games they play.*

Ego: *That's the point. You'll never know what she's up to.*
Some women have piece on the side just to 1-up you.
Some smell great and have stank attitudes.
Some look sweet and make back alley moves.

Clear: *I get it. Be out. I hear what you say about her.*
Ask Millie if she thinks I have reason to doubt her.

Ego: *Bring you proof? Um, I'm against it. Give it time.*
If you see Cash on the offensive, give him a short leash,
But keep him at a distance. This way, you can keep your eyes ,
On his intentions. If she keeps mentioning his name in conversations,
Repeatedly... That will give you half of the equation.
In the meantime, until you get the other half,
Hold back fears that they're involved like that.

Clear: I don't know if I can put this on pause like that.

Ego exits the gun range -

Ego: We're flawed like that, but don't let it get you.

I'm out. See you later. Keep your phone on and I'll hit you.

Clear declines a call from Diamond on his cell phone -

Aside -

Clear: If Diamond is doing me wrong how is that Ego's fault?

And if she is, I swear I'll have her body lined in chalk.

In front of all of New York, I'll dump her in the Hudson.

If she thinks this will slide, she doesn't know her husband.

To think my black heart fell for what I should've feared.

I let her eat through my armor and now my heart's pierced.

And look who's blowing me up. I should believe what?

It's always the beautiful ones that come and trip us up.

I can feel it in the air.

Audio #32 | **Act 3 Scene 3C**

Clear returns from the shooting range and enters the loft sorting mail. Diamond greets him with a smile. She reaches out to hug him and give him a kiss. He hugs her reluctantly and turns his head so that her kiss lands on his cheek. Watching from the living room, Millie sees Clear's response to Diamond. She shrugs it off and continues to read a magazine. Clear and Diamond turn to leave the apartment. Millie gets up from the couch to see them out into the hallway.

She watches as they board the elevator from the open apartment door. Diamond blows Millie a kiss goodbye as the elevator doors close. Millie shuts her hand as if she has caught Diamond's kiss and closes the door. She is surprised to find Diamond's phone sitting on the cushion next to her when she sits back on the couch. Soon after Diamond and Clear leave, Ego enters the apartment. Without noticing Millie sitting in the living room, he makes a beeline for the kitchen.

He pulls a container of juice from the fridge and takes a swig directly from the bottle. After a few long gulps he returns the container to the shelf. He is startled when he closes the refrigerator door to see Millie standing in the doorway of the kitchen. He finally acknowledges her while wiping his face with his sleeve like a defiant teen. She shakes her head in disgust and takes a seat back on the couch with her magazine. Ego walks over to the couch behind her and leans across the cushion where she is sitting. Millie closes her eyes and puckers her lips.

After a couple of seconds, she opens her eyes to find Ego searching for the remote control under the pillows around her. She frustratedly pulls him down onto the couch with her. Millie moves in close to Ego with Diamond's phone in her hand, holding it beneath her chin and smiling. Swaying back and forth like an innocent schoolgirl, she punches in the pass code "CLEAR" with the phone facing up so Ego can see it. Millie hands Ego the phone, then she gets up and grabs her bag so she can leave.

Ego hops up and races over to the front door. He opens the door for Millie but stands in front of it blocking her path. He asks Millie to keep his possession of the phone secret from Clear and Diamond for now. She dips under Ego's arm into the hall and pushes her upturned hand toward him. Ego stares blankly at her palm and then Millie re-extends her hand. Ego takes out his wallet and begins flipping through the money inside it.

Millie snatches the wallet from his hands and takes a black card from one of the folds. She then forcefully shoves the wallet into his chest. Ego fumbles to catch it before it drops to the floor. While he is off balance Millie pushes Ego back into the loft and slams the door. Ego revels in his possession of the phone and throws himself down on the couch to rest.

Audio #33 | *"Sour Candy"*

Clear enters his apartment looking despondent -

Diamond: Hey shooter. I hope your aim is on.

Because your timing is off. What happened?

Did you get lost? We're supposed to be at my video shoot.

That started an hour ago. I called to let you know.

But you didn't pick up your phone.

So let's keep it moving.

Clear: Not like I don't have more important things to be doing.

Diamond: Whose beef you been chewing?

Clear: I'm sorry. Did I snap?

I'm all over the map.

Forget it. That's my bad.

Diamond: Maybe this will make it better. It's so tight.

It's a picture that we took at the party from last night.

Clear: Not right now love. Look, we have to go.

Diamond drops her phone as she stands up from the couch -

Diamond: If you don't feel well, in the future, just say so.

See you later Millie. When you leave, please lock the door.

90

Diamond exits and Millie picks up the phone from the couch -

Millie: Oh, well now. What do we have here?

I bet you it's a whole bunch of pictures of her and Clear.

Ooooh look... Some old pictures of her and Cash.

I'll show this to my husband, I know it will take him back.

Enter Ego -

Ego: Hey! What's up with you? They left you here alone?

Millie: You see someone else home? I have something for you.

Ego: What? Another disease?

Millie: Yeah right. Please.

The only disease I can't get rid of is you.

Ego: Oh, you have the same problem? I married one too.

Millie: Forget you!!! Anyway, since we're all alone.

What can I get from you for a used cell phone?

Ego: Whose cell phone?

Millie: Um? Maybe Diamond's. The one she's always hiding.

The one you asked me to steal.

Ego: Are you for real?

Millie: She dropped it before she left.

And her password is C.L.E.A.R.

Not hard to forget.

Ego: Woman you are the best.

Millie: What do you want with it?

Ego: It's a surprise. Hand it over. Let me get it.

Millie: Get it back to me before she has time to miss it.

Remember that dress, all black, tightly fitted.

I'm on my way to Neiman Marcus now to go and get it.

Ego: Let's keep this a secret, stay quiet, and stick with it.

If you need me to be… a little more specific,

We know you have a big mouth.

On this let's zip it.

Audio #34 | **Act 3 Scene 3D**

Following Millie's departure from the apartment, Clear returns alone and obviously irritated. He storms across the loft and out onto the deck, barely acknowledging Ego resting on the couch. He sits on the edge of the whirlpool transfixed by the sunlight dancing around his reflection in the water. Ego follows him out onto the deck. Clear appears to be speaking out loud, but to no one in particular. He stops talking suddenly and pauses where he stands. Without warning Clear turns and lunges at Ego in a complete fit of rage.

In one swift motion Clear pulls Ego by the neck and drags him over to the whirlpool. He plunges Ego's face into the water. With little effort, he holds his head beneath the swirling bubbles for a few seconds and then pulls him back up. Ego comes up choking and gasping for air. Clear demands that Ego explain why he suspects Diamond of being unfaithful with Cash. Ego guilt trips Clear into listening to his reasons for bringing up Diamond's possible infidelity, calming him down slightly. Clear listens intently, enraged, confused and tortured by Ego's words.

Audio #35 | *"Something Unsaid"*

Ego looks through Diamond's phone -

Aside -

Ego: *I could use this to text Cash something explicit.*

Let him respond to it, thinking it's light flirting.

Show it to Clear break him down, and unnerve him.

I will fill his blood with poison until it hurts him,

And he starts to hate the taste of everything he loves.

Look at him now, not even half the man he was.

Less than 24 hours, his whole world sour.

Clear returns to the apartment alone -

Clear: *Women are such cowards.*

Ego: *Boss, don't lose your power. It's on you.*
She only does what you allow her.

Clear: *Leave them alone and you'll know, exactly what's yours.*
I'd rather have that, and be poor, than insecure.

Ego: *Be thankful for another day, leave the rest to the lord.*

Clear: *But outside of us, she never showed any lust. I'm talking,*
Super pure. Honestly, head to floor, Never saw, thought about it,
Been hurt by her or, suspected anything more than waking to her smile.

Ego: Sorry to hear that. This could hurt for a while.

Clear: I could be right next to the Giants locker room while,
She's doing her thing with the whole damn team.
It wouldn't bother me if I never knew anything about it,
Ever happening. Goodbye to that thought.
Goodbye to thinking I'm the reason why she walks that walk.
Goodbye to ambitious talk. Sign it off.
Goodbye to winning every fight before it's even fought.
Goodbye to us being on course ever again.

Ego: Why should you cave in? That's simply not you.

Clear grabs Ego by the collar and pushes him -

Clear: You got a point. You came to me and said,
"She wasn't true." Telling me all the things,
She supposedly might do. Who she might screw.
Now, show me some proof! Or I'm a turn rude boy,
"Tings about fi get koofe!" On everything I'm worth,
On this earth, my soul included, once we get into it,
Dog, there is no turning back! This reckless wrath,
Will leave you right here, breathless, on your back!

Ego: Why do me like that?

Clear and Ego walk out on to the apartment's private patio -

Clear: You need to make me see it.

Prove it! Make me believe it!

How did you come to conceive it?

Are you talking what you know?

Or did you think it, then perceived it? Give me answers!!

Or I'm taking your next breath before you breathe it!!!!!

Ego: I only got bits and pieces!

Clear briefly puts Ego's head into the water of the patio hot tub -

Clear: Don't confuse me with Jesus! No man on God's green earth,

Can say anything that he pleases, about me and mine,

And not end up resting in pieces!

Ego: I'm having trouble breathing! Give me a second. I need it!

When everyone warned me to be quiet, I didn't heed it!

I thought you had love for me, but that love has been defeated!

Clear: I'm sorry I got so heated. I know you didn't mean it.

Whatever you came across, I know you won't repeat it.

Ego: I'm between a rock and hard place.

I should turn a blind eye to ugliness in my face.

Clear*: I see your case. Maybe it's truth, maybe it's laced,*

But from day one, we've been as tight as Beyoncé and Jay.

Ego: *I'll try and get more info from the cats around the way.*

Clear throws a towel at Ego -

Clear: *There is no try. It's "do or die," and that's the only way.*

Ego: *You're telling me you want to see her dirt out on display?*

Clear: *If I do or if I don't, I'll be damned either way.*

Audio #36 | **Act 3 Scene 3E**

Shocked at his own actions Clear apologizes to Ego for his violent outburst. He tries to pull himself together, convinced that he has almost drowned a good friend for evil deeds that Cash and Diamond may have done. The two men walk back into the apartment. Clear disappears for a moment into the bathroom near the front door.

He returns with a towel. He tosses it at Ego and is captured by a glimpse of his angry reflection in the dining room mirror. Ego takes advantage of Clear's vulnerable state and encourages him to seek revenge on Diamond and Cash for betraying him. Now seething with anger, Ego has set Clear's mind on a path of undue vengeance against both his wife and best friend.

Audio #37 | "Mind Games"

Ego: Why can't they just obey? Listen to what we say.

Every woman's difficult from New York to the Bay.

They stick together like a pack of wolves. That's how they play.

Throwing salt in the game. Now tell me who's to blame.

If Diamond being a woman should fall into these things,

And bring them to your doorstep. Odds are long, I could be wrong.

It's not a sure bet.

Clear: I want a full report back. Is she loyal or not?

Give me everything you got.

Ego: Not to be a prick and even though it's not a lot.

I was hanging out with Cash, on the block just playing.

Out of nowhere he's like, "Diamond's kitten is banging."

Then he gets to saying how, "She's a sweet creature,

And Clear is not the only one who's seen her naked features."

Then he walked up on me like he was about to kiss me.

I'm thinking to myself, he must be messing with me.

Then he starts laughing and says, "Clear is going to get me.

Dismiss me, if I keep making jokes about his mistress."

Clear: Monstrous! Was anybody with you as a witness?

Ego: No. He called me out of the blue and said, "Let's kick it."

Clear: It sounds shady. Maybe he was teasing to begin with.

Ego: Maybe he was serious and hoping that I missed it.

Clear: You didn't. Like he won't miss the knife I slit his wrists with.

Ego: Maybe we can fix this. What about her phone?
Does Diamond try to sneak away and use it all alone?

Clear: Maybe so, but you know how it goes.
I'm rarely home.

Ego: I know Cash is always texting chicks,
He's trying to bone.

Clear: You're putting me in a zone.

Ego: A zone you need to be in.

Clear: She's not a human being. Enslaving me by deceiving.
I've cut people off at the legs for lesser reasons.
Made rich men break, and strong men, weaken.

Ego: Wait. Don't get too blown.

Clear: It's time to get it on.

Ego: Remember, we should think about this just in case you're wrong.

Clear: No, that ship is gone. Time for guns to get drawn.
The blood in my veins is now ice ,and flowing strong.
The cruise is over. I am now the storm after the calm.
I won't look back. I played it humble, and got bombed.
Anything I see that looks like love is getting harmed.
I vow from this point on, mark these words.
For Cash, vrrrat will be the only thing that's heard.

Ego: In broad day we'll bring the action to him like a verb.
Gun him down on the curb. If that's what must be done.
If someone must be "Ride or Die" for you, then I'm the one.
No remorse in this or this bloody business to come.

Clear: You know the business son.
You know the target and the name.
Next three days... I want Cash, smothered in flames.
Like De Niro in Untouchables, "I'll piss on his grave!"

Ego: He's dead at your request, but one hand we haven't played.
What about Diamond and getting back her good name?

Clear: *Damn her just the same. Damn her twice my pain.*

I want to kill her, bring her back, and then kill her again.

But I'll settle for once. For once she's done in.

Ego: *My oath is FOR EVER-EVER... Like Andre Benjamin.*

We've passed the point of no return.

Your name will be avenged my friend.

Clear: *I got my mind made up.*

AYATUL KURSI

"God – there is no deity except him,

The ever living, the sustainer of [all] existence.

Neither drowsiness overtakes him nor sleep.

To him belongs whatever is in the heavens,

And whatever is on the earth.

Who is it that can intercede with him except by his permission?

He knows what is [presently] before them and what will be after them,

And they encompass not a thing of his knowledge,

Except for what he wills.

His Kursi extends over the heavens and the earth,

And their preservation tires him not.

And he is the most high,

The most great."

Hip-Hop Verse

Shakespeare's

Othello

"WHEN THE KNIGHT FELL" V.1

CLEAR RISES

Intermission

Hip-Hop Verse Shakespeare's Othello

"WHEN THE KNIGHT FELL" V.1
CLEAR RISES

Available on Amazon:

Audible | Kindle | Hardcover

Audible Audiobook Includes:

Literary Musical + Audio Performances

Acapella + Spoken Word

Narrative + Instrumental

www.hiphopverseshakespeare.com

Audiobook Literary Musical Playlist   Act 1 | Scenes 1-5

Acapella + Spoken Word *"Halfway Shook"*

Acapella + Spoken Word *"A Clear Knight"*

Acapella + Spoken Word *"The Gathering"*

Acapella + Spoken Word *"No Angel"*

Acapella + Spoken Word *"Put Money On It"*

Audiobook Literary Musical Playlist   Act 2 | Scenes 6-11

Acapella + Spoken Word *"Homecoming"*

Acapella + Spoken Word *"Art of Words"*

Acapella + Spoken Word *"Still Shady"*

Acapella + Spoken Word *"NUZEE Luv Ballad"*

Acapella + Spoken Word *"Club Castle"*

Acapella + Spoken Word *"War Party"*

Audiobook Literary Musical Playlist   Act 3 | Scenes 12-18

Acapella + Spoken Word *"Jealous Never Worry"*

Acapella + Spoken Word *"Worry Less"*

Acapella + Spoken Word *"The Big Approach"*

Acapella + Spoken Word *"Thin Air"*

Acapella + Spoken Word *"Sour Candy"*

Acapella + Spoken Word *"Something Unsaid"*

Acapella + Spoken Word *"Mind Games"*

Audiobook Performance Playlist   Act 1 | Scenes 1-5

Narrative + Instrumental *"Halfway Shook"*

Narrative + Instrumental *"A Clear Knight"*

Narrative + Instrumental *"The Gathering"*

Narrative + Instrumental *"No Angel"*

Narrative + Instrumental *"Put Money On It"*

Audiobook Performance Playlist   Act 2 | Scenes 6-11

Narrative + Instrumental *"Homecoming"*

Narrative + Instrumental *"Art of Words"*

Narrative + Instrumental *"Still Shady"*

Narrative + Instrumental *"NUZEE Luv Ballad"*

Narrative + Instrumental *"Club Castle"*

Narrative + Instrumental *"War Party"*

Audiobook Performance Playlist   Act 3 | Scenes 12-18

Narrative + Instrumental *"Jealous Never Worry"*

Narrative + Instrumental *"Worry Less"*

Narrative + Instrumental *"The Big Approach"*

Narrative + Instrumental *"Thin Air"*

Narrative + Instrumental *"Sour Candy"*

Narrative + Instrumental *"Something Unsaid"*

Narrative + Instrumental *"Mind Games"*

Hip-Hop Verse

Shakespeare's

Othello

"WHEN THE KNIGHT FELL" V.2

CLEAR FALLS

AVAILABLE SOON

Made in the USA
Middletown, DE
17 June 2025